ON CLOUD
WINE
AF504577

MY DOCTOR SAYS
I NEED
GLASSES

SAVE WATER DRINK WINE

I MAKE
POUR
DECISIONS

I NEED TO
WINE
A LOT

OH LOOK!
IT'S
WINE
O'CLOCK

WINE
NOT?

SOMETIMES
I WINE
A LOT

MY
BLOOD
TYPE
IS
WINE-O

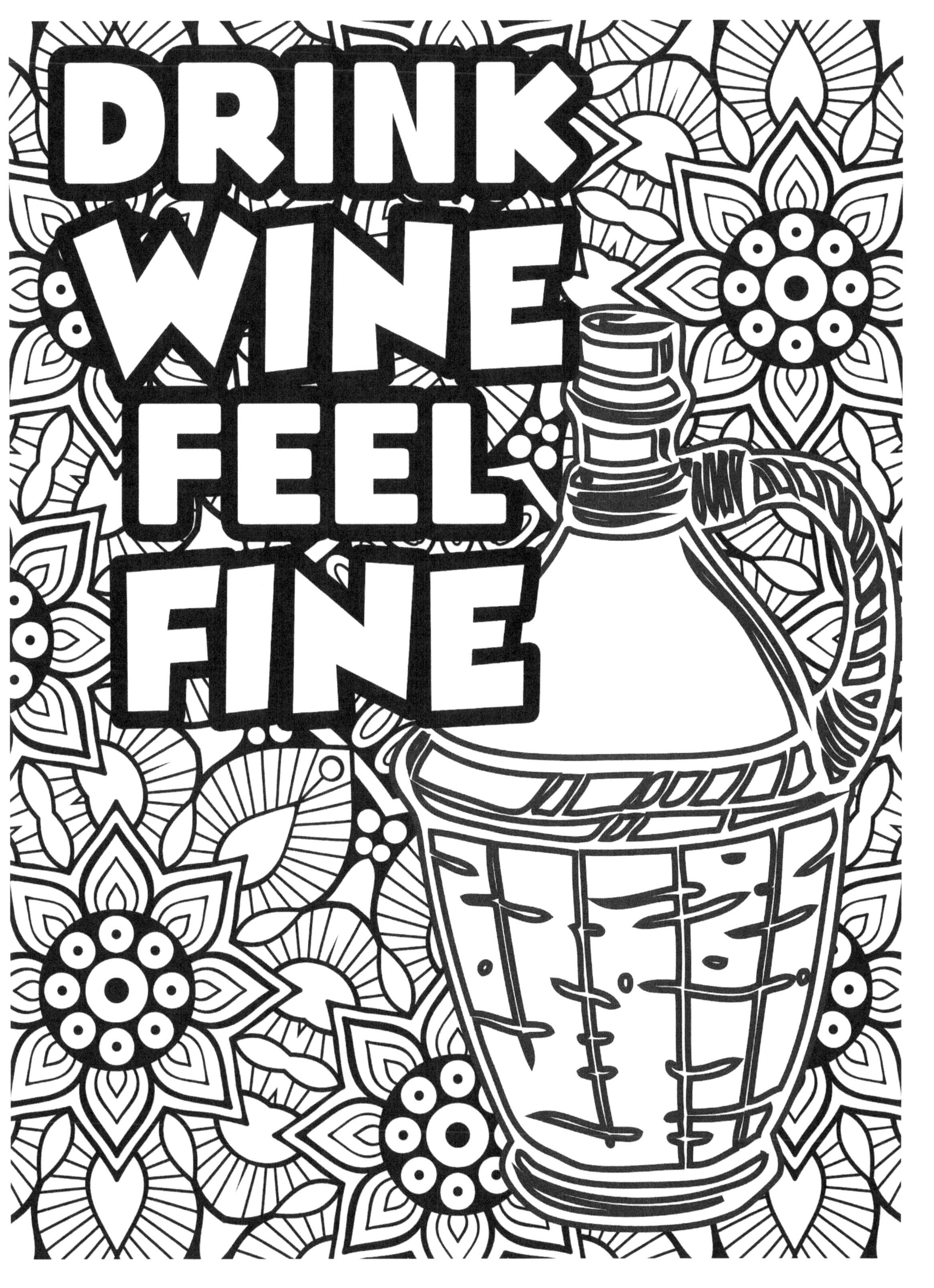

DRINK WINE FEEL FINE

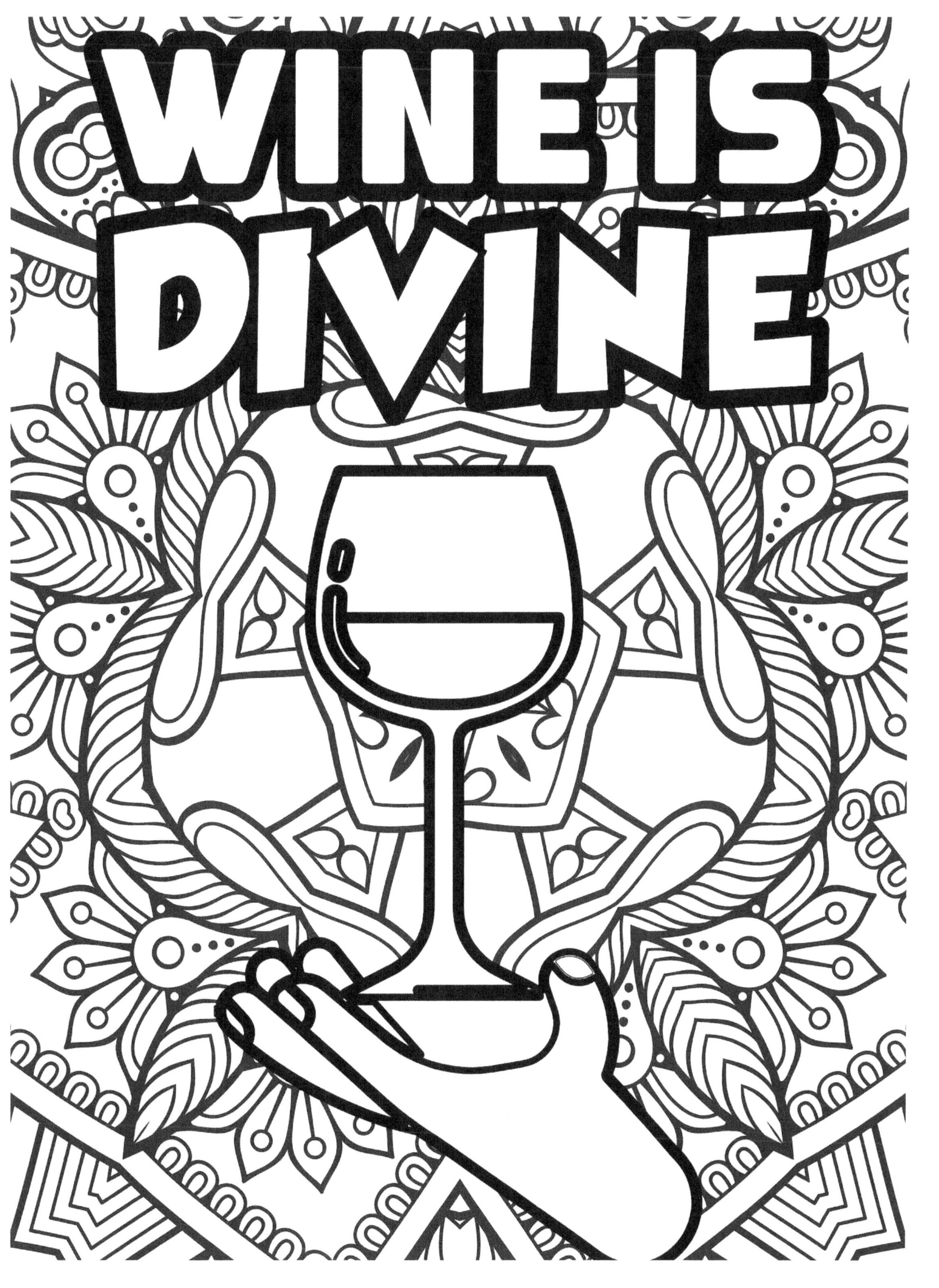

WINE IS
DIVINE

I PAIR WELL
WITH WINE

MY FAVORITE
DAY IS
WINESDAY

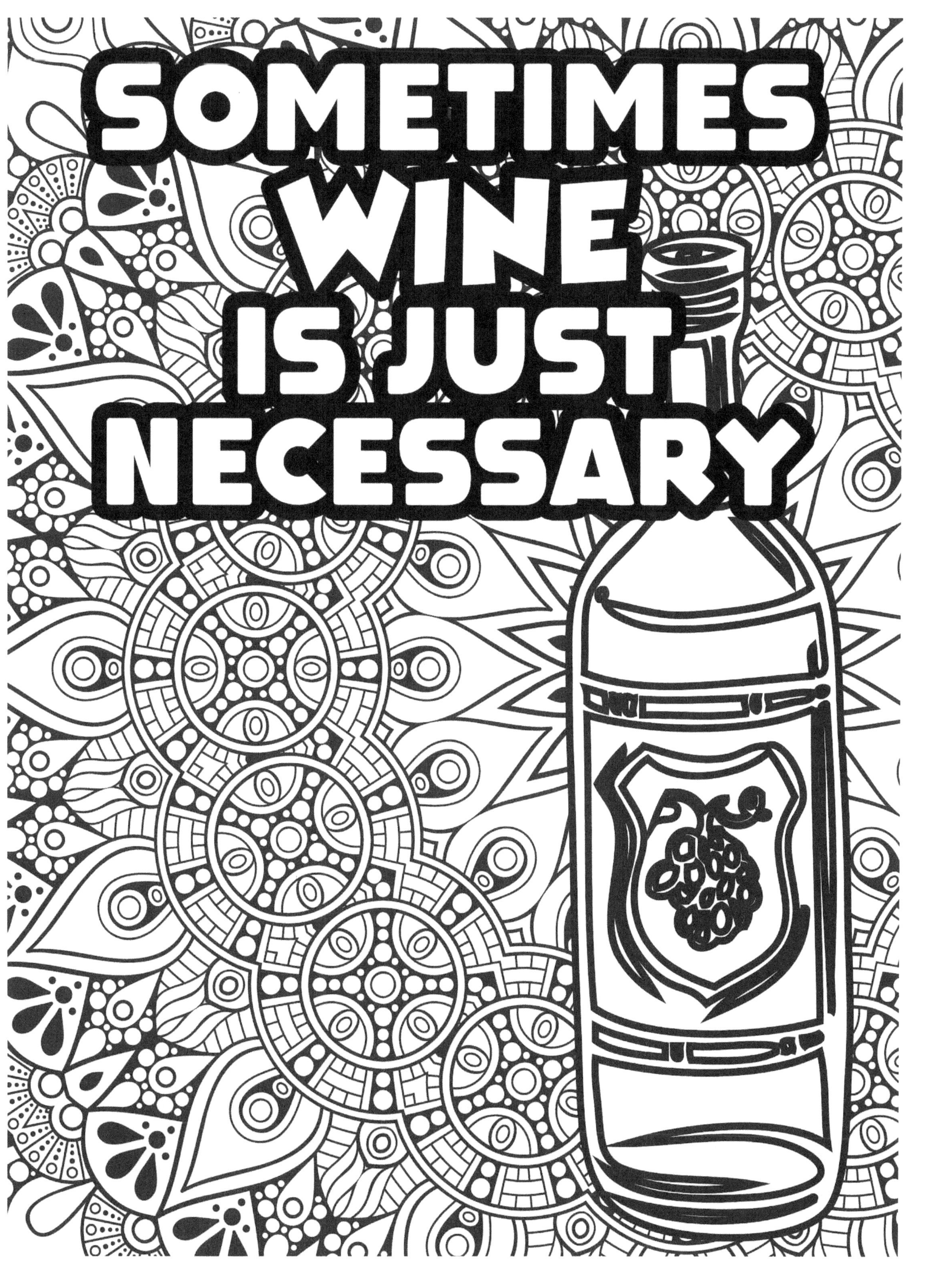

SOMETIMES WINE IS JUST NECESSARY

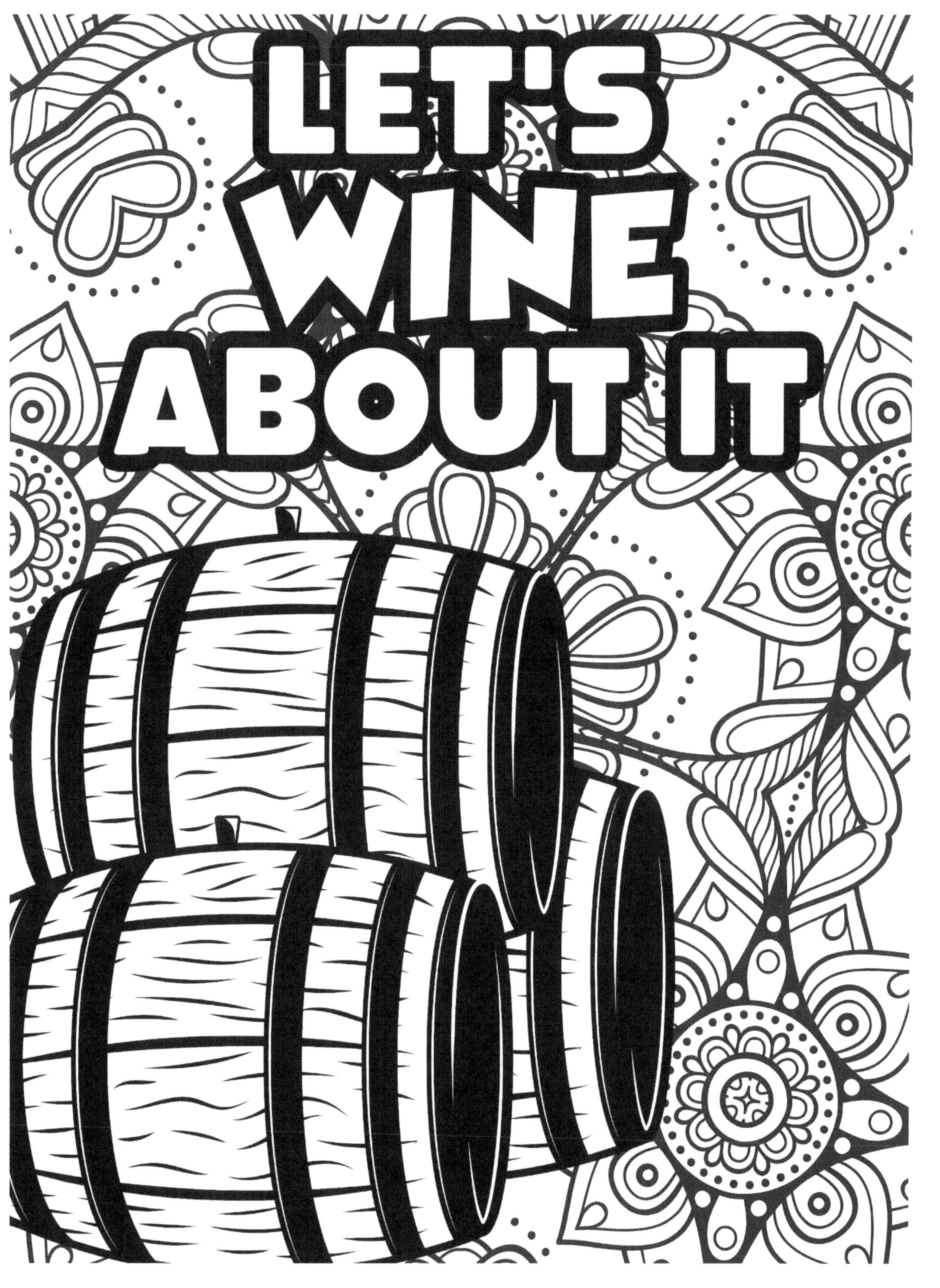

LET'S
WINE
ABOUT IT

WINE
JUICE WITH
MORE
LIFE
EXPERIENCE

THEY WHINE
I WINE

WINE
BECAUSE
ADULTING
IS HARD

WINE
A LITTLE
LAUGH
A LOT

LIFE IS TOO
SHORT
TO DRINK
BAD WINE